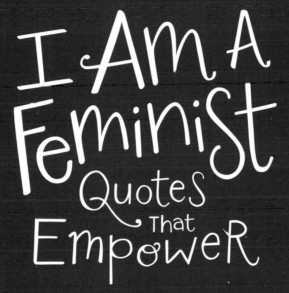

I Am A Feminist

Quotes That Empower

adamsmedia
Avon, Massachusetts

Published by
Adams Media, a division of F+W Media, Inc.
57 Littlefield Street, Avon, MA 02322. U.S.A.
www.adamsmedia.com

ISBN 10: 1-5072-0094-3
ISBN 13: 978-1-5072-0094-0
eISBN 10: 1-5072-0095-1
eISBN 13: 978-1-5072-0095-7

Printed in the United States of America.

10   9   8   7   6   5   4   3   2   1

Cover design by Stephanie Hannus.

*This book is available at quantity discounts for bulk purchases.
For information, please call 1-800-289-0963.*

Introduction

Empowered. Motivated. Inclusive.
Feminist.

Today's feminists are not afraid to speak their minds and let the world know what they want. And whether they're fighting for equality, looking to break through the glass ceiling, or trying to change the world, you can bet they're telling everyone who will listen—and some who won't—exactly what they believe in.

Here you'll find 200 quotes from a variety of past and present voices who will inspire, motive, and galvanize you to join the movement and add your voice to the fray, including:

Ruth Bader Ginsburg: "Women will have achieved true equality when men share with them the responsibility of bringing up the next generation."

Susan B. Anthony: "I declare to you that woman must not depend upon the protection of man, but must be taught to protect herself, and there I take my stand."

Beyoncé: "Your self-worth is determined by you. You don't have to depend on someone telling you who you are."

And today's feminism isn't just by women, for women anymore—and neither are the quotes throughout this book. Today men from all different walks of life—from Joss Whedon, John Legend, and Prince Harry to Joseph Gordon-Levitt, Bernie Sanders, and Barack Obama—are speaking up to show their support for their mothers, wives, daughters, friends, and women they've never even met.

Let the words of these men and women empower you … and add your words to this important conversation.

I am a woman and when I think, I must speak.

—*Beyoncé, pop star*

My mother told me to be a lady. And for her, that meant be your own person, be independent.

—Ruth Bader Ginsburg, associate justice, U.S. Supreme Court

The only advice I ever give women is: we want to support each other without distracting each other.

—Mindy Kaling, actor and author

I am an example of
what is possible when
girls from the very
beginning of their lives
are loved and nurtured
by people around them.
I was surrounded by
extraordinary women in
my life who taught me
about quiet strength and
dignity.

—Michelle Obama, first lady of the United States

I think it's like a disease that needs to be cured. And we could eradicate polio, I don't see why we can't eradicate misogyny.

—Alan Alda, actor

A woman without a man is like a fish without a bicycle.

—*Gloria Steinem, activist*

Don't allow men who hate women to define feminism as women who hate men.

—John Marcotte, activist

Women hold up half the sky.

—Chinese proverb

Let us no longer be imprisoned and defined by gender stereotypes or any stereotypes. Let us be defined by our individual actions, kindness, and decency to others. At the end of day, regardless of who you are, each and every individual deserves the opportunity to reach his or her full potential. Equality of the sexes is not merely an idea, but a birth-given right.

—*Rowan Blanchard, actor*

Confidence lets you pull anything off, even Tevas with socks.

—Lena Dunham, actor and author

I have a brain and a uterus, and I use both.

—Patricia Schroeder,
Colorado's first female member of Congress

I myself have never been able to find out precisely what feminism is: I only know that people call me a feminist whenever I express sentiments that differentiate me from a doormat or a prostitute.

—*Rebecca West, author, journalist, and literary critic*

I'm a woman
Phenomenally.
Phenomenal woman,
That's me.

—Maya Angelou, author

So, my unsolicited advice to women in the workplace is this. When faced with sexism or ageism or lookism or even really aggressive Buddhism, ask yourself the following question: "Is this person in between me and what I want to do?" If the answer is no, ignore it and move on. Your energy is better used doing your work and outpacing people that way. Then, when you're in charge, don't hire the people who were jerky to you.

—*Tina Fey, actor and author*

Womanhood is a whole different thing from girlhood. Girlhood is a gift ... Womanhood is a choice.

—Tori Amos, musician

It is starting to dawn on all women that it is time to forget about trying to compete with men who, with their blunders, have shown us that they have not been doing such a great job. Why try to equate ourselves with such flawed power?

—*Yoko Ono, artist, musician, activist*

Women must try to do things as men have tried. When they fail, their failure must be but a challenge to others.

—*Amelia Earhart, pilot*

I think you have to take the approach that feminism is ultimately about freedom.

—Tavi Gevinson, author

There cannot be true democracy unless women's voices are heard. There cannot be true democracy unless women are given the opportunity to take responsibility for their own lives. There cannot be true democracy unless all citizens are able to participate fully in the lives of their country.

—*Hillary Clinton, former secretary of state of the United States and presidential candidate*

Girls see these defined roles they're supposed to follow in life, but when I was a young child, my parents told me I could be anything.

—Joan Jett, musician

I only want to be acknowledged for having worked hard to build an equally significant audience and fan base to those of my peers. I believe the success of any woman should never be qualified by her gender.

—*Chelsea Handler, comedian*

Quite frankly I talk about the fact that I'm a feminist as often as I can, and every time I do it gets huge reaction and media reacts and the Twitterverse explodes and things like that, because here I am saying I'm a feminist. I will keep saying that until there is no more reaction to that when I say it, because that's where we want to get to.

—Justin Trudeau, prime minister of Canada

Whether it's nature, nurture, labels, or all of the above, there are certain traits that are traditionally associated with being a female. We are often called sensitive, emotional, and non-confrontational. Hey ladies, guess what? These all go into the "pro" column!

—*Kristen Bell, actor*

I would have girls regard themselves not as adjectives but nouns.

—Elizabeth Cady Stanton, American suffragist

I'm for gender equality because it should've never been any other way!

—Hugh Jackman, actor

I'm a feminist because I believe in women . . . it's a heavy word, feminism, but it's not one I think we should run from. I'm proud to be a feminist.

—*Sheryl Sandberg, executive, activist, and author*

The success of every woman should be the inspiration to another. We should raise each other up. Make sure you're very courageous: be strong, be extremely kind, and above all be humble.

—Serena Williams,
tennis player and Olympic medalist

As a woman, a lot of stories haven't been told and we've got a lot of catching up to do.

—Lili Taylor, actor

Women, if the soul of the nation is to be saved, I believe that you must become its soul.

—*Coretta Scott King, author and activist*

I demanded more rights for women because I know what women had to put up with.

—Eva Perón, former first lady of Argentina

It's really important for boys to see that girls take up half of the planet, which we do.

—Geena Davis, actor

What a man is is an arrow into the future and what a woman is is the place the arrow shoots off from.

—Sylvia Plath, author

The more I have spoken about feminism, the more I have realized that fighting for women's rights has too often become synonymous with man-hating. If there is one thing I know for certain, it is that has to stop. For the record, feminism, by definition, is the belief that men and women should have equal rights and opportunities. It is the theory of the political, economic, and social equality of the sexes.

—*Emma Watson, actor and activist*

Women are always at the front of revolutions.

—Buthayna Kamel,
Egypt's first female presidential candidate

A woman with a voice is, by definition, a strong woman.

—Melinda Gates, philanthropist

Yes, I'm a feminist, because I see all women as smart, gifted, and tough.

—Zaha Hadid, architect and Pritzker Architecture Prize winner

I hope that by speaking today, you
absorbed a small amount of light,
a small knowing that you can't be
silenced, a small satisfaction that justice
was served, a small assurance that
we are getting somewhere, and a big,
big knowing that you are important,
unquestionably, you are untouchable,
you are beautiful, you are to be valued,
respected, undeniably, every minute
of every day, you are powerful and
nobody can take that away from you.
To girls everywhere, I am with you.

—*Anonymous sexual assault victim advocate*

I desire you would Remember the Ladies, and be more generous and favourable to them than your ancestors. Do not put such unlimited power into the hands of the Husbands.

—*Abigail Adams,*
former first lady of the United States

I'll smile when I want to and having a strange old man tell me to isn't a good reason.

—Mo Welch, comedian

I had gone from believing that women's issues were a distraction, mere ancillary problems to be addressed after everything else had been taken care of, to the realization that women are the issue, the *core* issue. We will fail to solve any problem—poverty, peace, sustainable development, environment, health—unless we look at it through a gender lens and make sure the solution will be good for women.

—*Jane Fonda, actor and activist*

I like stories where women save themselves.

—Neil Gaiman, author

Some women choose to follow men, and some women choose to follow their dreams. If you're wondering which way to go, remember that your career will never wake up and tell you that it doesn't love you anymore.

—Lady Gaga, pop star

We are not going back.
Not only are we not going to
retreat on women's rights, we
are going to expand them.
We are going forward,
not backward.

—Bernie Sanders,
U.S. senator and former presidential candidate

It seems that life is not easy for any of us. But what of that? We must have perseverance and above all confidence in ourselves. We must believe that we are gifted for something, and that this thing, at whatever cost, must be attained.

—Marie Curie, scientist

A man told me that for a woman, I was very opinionated. I said, "for a man you're kind of ignorant."

—Anne Hathaway, actor

The most courageous act is still to think for yourself. Aloud.

—Coco Chanel, fashion designer

To call woman the weaker sex is a libel; it is man's injustice to woman. If by strength is meant brute strength, then, indeed, is woman less brute than man. If by strength is meant moral power, then woman is immeasurably man's superior. Has she not greater intuition, is she not more self-sacrificing, has she not greater powers of endurance, has she not greater courage? Without her, man could not be. If nonviolence is the law of our being, the future is with woman. Who can make a more effective appeal to the heart than woman?

—*Mahatma Gandhi, Indian nationalist and pacifist*

Whatever you choose, however many roads you travel, I hope that you choose not to be a lady. I hope you will find some way to break the rules and make a little trouble out there. And I also hope that you will choose to make some of that trouble on behalf of women.

—*Nora Ephron, author*

Whatever women do, they must do twice as well as men to be thought half as good. Luckily, this is not difficult.

—*Charlotte Whitton, first female mayor of Ottawa*

I do not wish [women] to have power over men; but over themselves.

—Mary Shelley, author

To me, the tragedy about this whole image-obsessed society is that young girls get so caught up in just achieving that they forget to realize that they have so much more to offer the world.

—*America Ferrera, actor*

Your self-worth is determined by you. You don't have to depend on someone telling you who you are.

—*Beyoncé, pop star*

I believe it's a woman's right to decide what she wants to wear and if a woman can go to the beach and wear nothing, then why can't she also wear everything?

—*Malala Yousafzai, activist*

Women will have achieved true equality when men share with them the responsibility of bringing up the next generation.

—Ruth Bader Ginsburg, associate justice, U.S. Supreme Court

I love to see a young girl go out and grab the world by the lapels. Life's a bitch. You've got to go out and kick ass.

—Maya Angelou, author

Does feminist mean large unpleasant person who'll shout at you, or does feminist mean someone who believes women are human beings? If it's the latter, I'll sign up.

—Margaret Atwood, author

I have an independent streak. You know, it's kind of hard to tell a[n] independent woman what to do.

—Betty Ford, former first lady of the United States and activist

Wherever there is a human being, I see God-given rights inherent in that being, whatever may be the sex or complexion.

—*William Lloyd Garrison, abolitionist and journalist*

Every individual matters.
Every individual has a role
to play. Every individual
makes a difference.

—Jane Goodall, scientist and animal rights activist

Women are fifty-one
percent of humankind.
Empowering them will
change everything.
I can promise you
that. Women working
together, linked,
informed, and educated
can bring peace and
prosperity to this
forsaken land.

—*Isabel Allende, author*

As a woman, I find it very embarrassing to be in a meeting and realize I'm the only one in the room with balls.

—Rita Mae Brown, author

One is not born,
but rather becomes,
a woman.

—*Simone de Beauvoir, author and political activist*

I don't know what it's like to be a woman in a band—I have nothing else to compare it to. But I will say that I doubt in the history of rock journalism and writing any man has been asked, "Why are you in an all-man band?"

—Carrie Brownstein, musician, author, actor, and comedian

I really think that there was a great advantage in many ways to being a woman. I think we are a lot better at personal relationships, and then have the capability obviously of telling it like it is when it's necessary.

—Madeleine Albright, first female secretary of state of the United States and diplomat

Feminism didn't die, but it didn't thrive either. It just survived, heroically optimistic as ever. We believe in the best of ourselves; we believe in the best of men.

—Beatrix Campbell, author

When you feel powerful, you are willing to stand up for your rights, you are willing to stand up for what you believe in, you're more willing to stand up and be counted.

—*Margaret Cho, comedian*

Women are the real architects of society.

—Harriet Beecher Stowe, abolitionist and author

I hope that I inspire
women to believe
in themselves, no
matter where they
come from; no matter
what education they
have; what particular
background they
originate from.

—Madonna, pop star

We've begun to raise daughters more like sons . . . but few have the courage to raise our sons more like our daughters.

—Gloria Steinem, activist

All women are feminists at heart. In their psychology lies a great love for women as a class.

—Ann Oakley, author

I have chosen to no longer be apologetic for my femaleness and my femininity. And I want to be respected in all of my femaleness because I deserve to be.

—*Chimamanda Ngozi Adichie, author*

First and foremost, I'm a feminist. And basically that stems from a strong belief that all people and creatures deserve equal opportunity, rights, and respect.

—Kathy Najimy, actor

I am no bird; and
no net ensnares me;
I am a free human
being, with an
independent will.

—Charlotte Brontë, author

It takes years as a woman to unlearn what you have been taught to be sorry for. It takes years to find your voice and seize your real estate.

—Amy Poehler, actor and author

I am not free while any woman is unfree, even when her shackles are very different from my own.

—Audre Lorde, author and activist

We all fight over what the label "feminism" means, but for me it's about empowerment. It's not about being more powerful than men—it's about having equal rights with protection, support, justice. It's about very basic things. It's not a badge like a fashion item.

—Annie Lennox, musician

There are a lot of people who say, "Yeah yeah, I'm a feminist," and they're not, actually. I wouldn't want to throw that word around, because it's a very strong thing.

—Saoirse Ronan, actor

There is no limit to what we, as women, can accomplish.

—*Michelle Obama, first lady of the United States*

My hope for the future, not just in the music industry, but in every young girl I meet … is that they all realize their worth and ask for it.

—Taylor Swift, pop star

Women have lived through a world where backward-looking ideologies try to interfere with the basic health decisions made by a woman and her doctor. And we are not going back. Not now, not ever.

—Elizabeth Warren, U.S. senator

I'm tough, ambitious, and I know exactly what I want. If that makes me a bitch, OK.

—Madonna, pop star

The most important lesson I think I could impart is don't let anyone determine what your horizons are going to be. You get to determine those yourself. The only limitations are whatever particular talents you happen to have and how hard you're willing to work. And if you let others define who you ought to be, or what you ought to be because they put you in a category, they see your race, they see your gender and they put you in a category. You shouldn't let that happen.

—Condoleezza Rice,
former secretary of state of the United States

We must tell girls
their voices are
important.

—Malala Yousafzai, activist

I have an overactive sense of justice. I want women to realize you don't have to work for the company. You can run the company. I want the scope for them to be endless.

—Melissa McCarthy, actor

If the first woman God ever made was strong enough to turn the world upside down all alone, these women together ought to be able to turn it back, and get it right side up again! And now they is asking to do it, the men better let them.

—*Sojourner Truth, abolitionist*

For most people, being a feminist just sounds so *complicated*. It's always more convenient to not be someone with controversial opinions.

—Tavi Gevinson, author

Women, unless they were quite wealthy, have always worked: in the house and out of the house, on the farm, in factories, sometimes caring for other people's kids, often leaving their own under Grandma's practiced eye.

—*Barbara Kingsolver, author*

Some people ask: "Why the word feminist? Why not just say you are a believer in human rights, or something like that?" Because that would be dishonest. Feminism is, of course, part of human rights in general—but to choose to use the vague expression human rights is to deny the specific and particular problem of gender. It would be a way of pretending that it was not women who have, for centuries, been excluded.

—*Chimamanda Ngozi Adichie, author*

I hate to hear you talking . . . as if women were all fine ladies, instead of rational creatures. We none of us expect to be in smooth water all our days.

—Jane Austen, author

Don't waste your energy trying to educate or change opinions. Go "Over! Under! Through!" and opinions will change organically when you're the boss. Or they won't. Who cares? Do your thing, and don't care if they like it.

—*Tina Fey, actor and author*

I think the key is for women not to set any limits.

—Martina Navratilova, tennis player

I do call myself a feminist. Absolutely! It's worth paying attention to the roles that are sort of dictated to us, and that we don't have to fit into those roles. We can be anybody we want to be.

—Joseph Gordon-Levitt, actor

People say, "Gee, you don't really do political music." Well, I sing a lot of songs about how men and women and lovers treat each other, and none of us want to be talked down to or belittled or ignored or disrespected … So I'm proud to be a feminist.

—*Bonnie Raitt, musician*

When you've worked hard, and done well, and walked through that doorway of opportunity, you do not slam it shut behind you.
You reach back.

—*Michelle Obama, first lady of the United States*

It's not about women acting like men, it's about women acting like women and being successful.

—Zooey Deschanel, actor

We have a hunger of the mind which asks for knowledge of all around us, and the more we gain, the more is our desire; the more we see, the more we are capable of seeing.

—Maria Mitchell, first female professional astronomer in the United States

I declare to you that woman must not depend upon the protection of man, but must be taught to protect herself, and there I take my stand.

—Susan B. Anthony, social reformer

Well-behaved women seldom make history.

—Laurel Thatcher Ulrich, American historian

We know that when women are empowered, they immeasurably improve the lives of everyone around them—their families, their communities, and their countries. This is not just about women; we men need to recognize the part we play too. Real men treat women with dignity and give them the respect they deserve.

—*Prince Harry of Wales*

Girls face so many challenges—people are constantly telling them they can't do things, they can't be funny, they can't run the companies—but my advice is just not to focus on anyone telling you that you can't do anything, or politics in your situation … Just think about your art, that thing you're gonna do.

—*Mindy Kaling, actor and author*

Young women should pave their own path. I find it quite confining to live up to anybody else's expectations of who you should be.

—Jessica Alba, actor

Love yourself first and everything else falls into line. You really have to love yourself to get anything done in this world.

—Lucille Ball, actor and comedian

A woman is like a tea bag—you never know how strong she is until she gets in hot water.

—*Unknown*

When a man gives his opinion, he's a man. When a woman gives her opinion, she's a bitch.

—Bette Davis, actor

Women are the only exploited group in history to have been idealized into powerlessness.

—Erica Jong, author

For what is done or learned by one class of women becomes, by virtue of their common womanhood, the property of all women.

—*Elizabeth Blackwell,*
first female physician in the United States

My coach said I ran like a girl, I said if he could run a little faster he could too.

—Mia Hamm, soccer player and Olympic medalist

I think the degree of a nation's civilisation may be measured by the degree of enlightenment of its women.

—Helen Keller, author and activist

Other people will call me a rebel, but I just feel like I'm living my life and doing what I want to do. Sometimes people call that rebellion, especially when you're a woman.

—Joan Jett, musician

[A] woman should have every honorable motive to exertion which is enjoyed by man, to the full extent of her capacities and endowments. The case is too plain for argument. Nature has given woman the same powers, and subjected her to the same earth, breathes the same air, subsists on the same food, physical, moral, mental, and spiritual. She has, therefore, an equal right with man, in all efforts to obtain and maintain a perfect existence.

—Frederick Douglass, abolitionist

We need to get women to the point where they aren't apologizing. It's time to take ownership in our success.

—*Tory Burch, CEO and designer*

We need policies for long-term security that are designed by women, focused on women, executed by women—not at the expense of men, or instead of men, but alongside and with men. There is no greater pillar of stability than a strong, free and educated woman, and there is no more inspiring role model than a man who respects and cherishes women and champions their leadership.

—*Angelina Jolie, actor and activist*

In the future, there will be no female leaders. There will just be leaders.

—Sheryl Sandberg, executive, activist, and author

There's nothing wrong with being a strong woman. For me, that's what I try to let young women know: You can be strong and you can be intense, and that's fine. You don't have to be a girl that's an athlete, you can just be an athlete.

—*Skylar Diggins, basketball player*

[You] have what it takes to be a victorious, independent, fearless woman.

—Tyra Banks, model and TV personality

There are many women who came before me who didn't really have the same opportunities that I have had. That's why I always wanted to be a great ambassador—not only today's generation—but for the women who really didn't have a voice, but who paved the way for me.

—Jackie Joyner-Kersee, track-and-field athlete and Olympic medalist

It's about being alive, and feisty, and NOT sitting down and shutting up. Even though people would like you to.

—Pink, pop star

Be yourself, because if you can get away with it, that is the ultimate feminist act.

—Liz Phair, musician

Michelle and I have raised our daughters to speak up when they see a double standard or feel unfairly judged based on their gender or race—or when they notice that happening to someone else. It's important for them to see role models out in the world who climb to the highest levels of whatever field they choose. And yes, it's important that their dad is a feminist, because now that's what they expect of all men.

—*Barack Obama, president of the United States*

We wouldn't do group interviews. If we found out it was a piece on women in rock, we wouldn't do it because we felt like we deserved our own place, our own article, without being lumped in by gender.

—Donita Sparks, musician

Solidarity is based on the principle that we are willing to put ourselves at risk to protect each other.

—Starhawk (Miriam Simos), author and activist

I call myself a feminist when people ask me if I am, and of course I am 'cause it's about equality, so I hope everyone is. You know you're working in a patriarchal society when the word feminist has a weird connotation.

—Ellen Page, actor

The people who could do most to improve the situation of so many women and children are in fact men. It's in our hands to stop violence towards women.

—Patrick Stewart, actor

The most common way people give up their power is by thinking they don't have any.

—Alice Walker, author

Q: So, why do you write these strong female characters?

A: Because you're still asking me that question.

—Joss Whedon, screenwriter and director

To be a feminist is to integrate an ideology of equality and female empowerment into the very fiber of my life. It is to search for personal clarity in the midst of systemic destruction, to join in sisterhood with women when often we are divided, to understand power structures with the intention of challenging them.

—Rebecca Walker, author

Men, their rights, and nothing more; women, their rights, and nothing less.

—Susan B. Anthony, social reformer

Too many women throw themselves into romance because they're afraid of being single, then start making compromises and losing their identity. I won't do that.

—Julie Delpy, *actor*

A huge part of being a feminist is giving other women the freedom to make choices you might not necessarily make yourself.

—Lena Dunham, actor and author

My idea of feminism is self-determination, and it's very open-ended: every woman has the right to become herself, and do whatever she needs to do.

—Ani DiFranco, musician and activist

The whole world is starting to realize that it was the most unwise thing for our society to have ignored women power, to run the society with male priorities.

—Yoko Ono, artist, musician, and activist

I really do like being independent, and I don't want to have to rely on anyone else to cart me around if I break a bone.

—Blythe Danner, actor

No man is good enough to govern any woman without her consent.

—Susan B. Anthony, social reformer

You can't just sit there and wait for people to give you that golden dream. You've got to get out there and make it happen for yourself.

—*Diana Ross, musician*

[A]s a woman, I have no country. As a woman I want no country. As a woman my country is the whole world.

—Virginia Woolf, author

I could not, at any age, be content to take my place by the fireside and simply look on. Life was meant to be lived. Curiosity must be kept alive. One must never, for whatever reason, turn his back on life.

—Eleanor Roosevelt,
former first lady of the United States

We all require and want respect, man or woman, black or white. It's our basic human right.

—*Aretha Franklin, musician*

Feminism is not just about women; it's about letting all people lead fuller lives.

—Jane Fonda, actor and activist

As for my girls, I'll raise them to think they breathe fire.

—Jessica Kirkland, author

I'm not ashamed to dress like a woman because I don't think it's shameful to be a woman.

—Iggy Pop, musician

I've always been of the mindset that you shouldn't wait for anyone to give you the opportunities you want, you should just make the opportunities yourself.

—*Tuesday Bassen, artist*

You know, it's just important to be a good ally. There's nothing friendlier towards injustice than silence.

—*Amani Al-Khatahtbeh, author and activist*

We can push ourselves further. We always have more to give.

—*Simone Biles, gymnast and Olympic medalist*

Women are each other's Wonderbras: uplifting, supportive, and making each other look bigger and better.

—*Kathy Lette, author*

Can you imagine a world without men? No crime, and lots of fat, happy women.

—Nicole Hollander, cartoonist

Honor your daughters. They are honorable.

—Malala Yousafzai, activist

He—and if there is a God,
I am convinced he is a
he, because no woman
could or would ever fuck
things up this badly.

—*George Carlin, comedian*

Women are complicated, women are multifaceted—not because women are crazy, but because people are crazy, and women happen to be people.

—Tavi Gevinson, author

Let me take a minute to say that I love bossy women. Some people hate the word, and I understand how "bossy" can seem like a shitty way to describe a woman with a determined point of view, but for me, a bossy woman is someone to search out and celebrate.

—*Amy Poehler, actor and author*

I see my body as an instrument, rather than an ornament.

—Alanis Morissette, musician

Women have to harness their power—it's absolutely true. It's just learning not to take the first no. And if you can't go straight ahead, you go around the corner.

—Cher, pop star

If you believe that men and women have equal rights, if someone asks if you're feminist, you have to say yes because that is how words work. You can't be like, "Oh yeah, I'm a doctor that primarily does diseases of the skin." Oh, so you're a dermatologist? "Oh no, that's way too aggressive of a word! No, no, not at all; not at all."

—*Aziz Ansari, actor*

The especial genius of women I believe to be electrical in movement, intuitive in function, spiritual in tendency.

—Margaret Fuller, author

It is absolutely men's responsibility to fight sexism too. And as spouses and partners and boyfriends, we need to work hard and be deliberate about creating truly equal relationships.

—*Barack Obama, president of the United States*

Stop telling girls they can be anything they want when they grow up. I think it's a mistake. Not because they can't, but because it would've never occurred to them they couldn't.

—*Sarah Silverman, actor and comedian*

Some of us are becoming the men we wanted to marry.

—Gloria Steinem, activist

So if diva means giving your best, then yes, I guess I am a diva.

—*Patti LaBelle, musician*

I so believe that older women have tremendous value to their families, their community, their country, the world.

—*Sally Field, actor*

I don't dress up for boys.
I dress up to stare at my
reflection as I walk by
store windows.

I believe that the rights of women and girls is the unfinished business of the 21st century.

—Hillary Clinton, *former secretary of state of the United States and presidential candidate*

I don't care what you think about me. I don't think about you at all.

—Coco Chanel, fashion designer

I'm a feminist. I've been a female for a long time now. It'd be stupid not to be on my own side.

—Maya Angelou, author

Feminism is the radical notion that women are human beings.

—Cheris Kramarae, author

To the women of my beloved country: believe in yourselves. You are strong. Speak up about your dreams and your goals every day so that everyone knows that you exist and you have the right to choose.

—*Sonita Alizadeh, rapper and activist*

I do think because women are so clever and flexible and such good communicators, it has been hard for men to evolve and keep up. I think we could do a little better to help them out.

—*Rashida Jones, actor*

I'm not going to limit myself just because people won't accept the fact that I can do something else.

—Dolly Parton, musician

Sentences that begin with "all women" are never, never true.

—Margaret Culkin Banning, author

I've always believed that one woman's success can only help another woman's success.

—*Gloria Vanderbilt, artist and author*

If you're going to generalize about women, you'll find yourself up to here in exceptions.

—Dolores Hitchens, author

Women are not a special interest group in the usual sense of the term. We are half the population.

—Virginia Carabillo, former vice president, National Organization for Women

Girls do what their mothers tell them. Ladies do what society tells them. Women make up their own minds.

—*Karen Kijewski, author*

Anything's possible if you've got enough nerve.

—J.K. Rowling, author

When a man hits a target, they call him a marksman. When I hit a target, they call it a trick. Never did like that much.

—*Annie Oakley, sharpshooter*

You wanna fly, you got to give up the shit that weighs you down.

—*Toni Morrison, author*

Being a feminist is not how other people treat you, it's how you treat other people.

—*Michele Kort, author*

Woman's cause is one and universal.

—Anna Julia Cooper, author

When we talk about equal rights, there are issues that face women disproportionately . . . If your son can do it, your daughter should be able to.

—*Beyoncé, pop star*

I think it is right that as a woman I am paid the same as my male counterparts. I think it is right that I should be able to make decisions about my own body. I think it is right that women be involved on my behalf in the policies and decision-making of my country. I think it is right that socially I am afforded the same respect as men.

—*Emma Watson, actor and activist*

It just made more sense to me to be a feminist than to not be a feminist.

—*Tavi Gevinson, author*

I am not telling men
to step away from
speaking for women's
rights; rather, I am
focusing on women to
be independent to fight
for themselves.

—*Malala Yousafzai, activist*

Every great dream begins with a dreamer. Always remember, you have within you the strength, the patience, and the passion to reach for the stars to change the world.

—*Harriet Tubman, abolitionist*

You can be a thousand different women. It's your choice which one you want to be. It's about freedom and sovereignty. You celebrate who you are. You say, "This is my kingdom."

—*Salma Hayek, actor*

I say if I'm beautiful.
I say if I'm strong.
You will not determine
my story—I will.

—Amy Schumer, actor and comedian

How wrong it is for woman to expect the man to build the world she wants, rather than set out to create it herself.

—Anaïs Nin, author

We [women] are half
the sky and the world.
We are a very important
energy that the society
can use. To denigrate
us or to abuse us or to
sweep us under the rug
is not beneficial for the
society itself.

—*Yoko Ono, artist, musician, and activist*

There will never be
a new world order
until women are
a part of it.

—*Alice Paul, suffragist*

A liberated woman is one who has sex before marriage and a job after.

—*Gloria Steinem, activist*

We all are in a physical body with beating hearts, with compassion and love. We are all seekers, we all want questions, we all want fulfillment, we want to live our best lives. We want to be healthy and happy and squeeze the most that we can out of life. I think that's all women.

—Gwyneth Paltrow, actor

Never ever accept "because you are a woman" as a reason for doing or not doing anything.

—Chimamanda Ngozi Adichie, author

Sisterhood is powerful.

—Kathie Sarachild, activist

My hardcore badass feminist mom told both my brother and me that we were feminists from the time we were like two years old, so if she ever heard me saying I wasn't a feminist she'd fly to my house and smack me upside the head.

—John Green, author

We are the ones we've been waiting for.

—June Jordan, poet

It's a wise man that understands that no two women are alike.

—*Elinor Macartney Lane, author*

You should always speak your mind and be bold and obnoxious and do whatever you want and don't let anybody tell you to stop it.

—Chelsea Handler, comedian

You don't have to be anti-man to be pro-woman.

—Jane Galvin Lewis, author and activist

Feminism isn't about making women stronger. Women are already strong. It's about changing the way the world perceives that strength.

—*G.D. Anderson, author*

Here's to strong women.
May we know them.
May we be them.
May we raise them.

—*Unknown*

There is no female mind. The brain is not an organ of sex. Might as well speak of the female liver.

—*Charlotte Perkins Gilman, author and activist*

All men should be feminists. If men care about women's rights, the world will be a better place. We are better off when women are empowered. It leads to a better society.

—*John Legend, musician*

I would hope everyone would be a feminist.

—Mia Wasikowska, actor